THE LIFE OF AN ADDICT

Greggory Davis

Dedication Page

This book is dedicated to my loving family, Parents (Gary and Elaine Davis) and my brothers (Jeffery and Ronald Davis). They continued to love me even in the darkest days of my addiction, when I didn't love myself. Thank you for never giving up on me and for believing in me. I am so blessed to have all of you in my life. Mom you have always been my rock and I can't ever say it enough I Love You.

Also, to God who protected me and kept me alive during my addiction. Without God I would not be where I am today.

Acknowledgement

This book of poetry was inspired by my tragic events in my darkest days of addiction. There were assaults, sexual assaults, life on the streets and the deaths of many people that I associated with from drug overdoses.

There are several great people in my life today that were major parts of my recovery and I feel that they went over and above their duties to help me find myself and to begin healing and loving myself today. Sean M., Beth W., and Gail A. all loved me from the beginning of my time in rehab and made it ok for me to face my demons, and move forward the amazing life I have today.

Contents

Why Me

The day we met was magical
Your love seemed all so real
And my heart I gave to you.
Soon your beatings started
In your quest to gain control
Of an innocent boy of 12.
You introduced me to alcohol,
Weed and even heroin.
You made a bad drug deal
And gave me up to them
To pay your debt sexually.

I had come to fear you
Your abuse only continued to get worse
Yet I loved you through it all.
One night I found you on the floor
With a needle deep in your arm,
Your pulse was barley there,
You were barely hanging on.
I just sat down and cried
While I held your hand
As you slowly slipped away.
After eight long years
I was left to say good bye.

Greggory Davis

The Sun Will Rise

My path in life was so dark.
There was no sun to light my way
Through the dark and lonely streets
That I was traveling down.
Addicted to drugs and alcohol,
I was just a major train wreck
Waiting to take place.

Insanity ran so deep
In my Shattered view of reality.
The good times passed me by
And the bad shit continued on.
I only wanted to truly die
And end the horrible pain.
But I was too damned scared.
I don't know way God held me
Securely in his arms, while
Continuing to spare my life.

Today my life is so much brighter
And in my heart is new hope'
This all began at "the sunrise center"
Where the sun will rise
Through my darkest day.

Greggory Davis

The Search

I have always stood
On the outside of life
Just longing to fit in.
It's really sad to look back
And see a 12 year old boy
Who just couldn't fit in.
No matter how hard he tried.
He tried sports, and scouts,
This group and that group.
But sadly enough
He just didn't fit in.
At every turn in life,
Rejection seemed to be right there.
When he had lost all hope,
And knew in his heart
That he'd never fit in,
A group of misfits accepted him in.
The introduced him
To week, beer and heroin.
Finally his search was over
And he found he fit in.

Greggory Davis

The Prince of Death

He comes into my dreams,
My life and soul is what he wants.
He laughs, he teases and
Calls me out my name.
"Come on you fucking Junkie,
It's time to go get high."
After all he knows
That I am really not that shy.
You name the game, he says
Then we'll go get high.

My soul is what he is after now
And if I quit the game,
He will chase me down and
Haunt my darkest dreams again.
Until in fear, I will use again.
Now I have seen and done it all
He was, he is, and will always be
"The Prince of death
Who only wants my
Fucking soul.

Greggory Davis

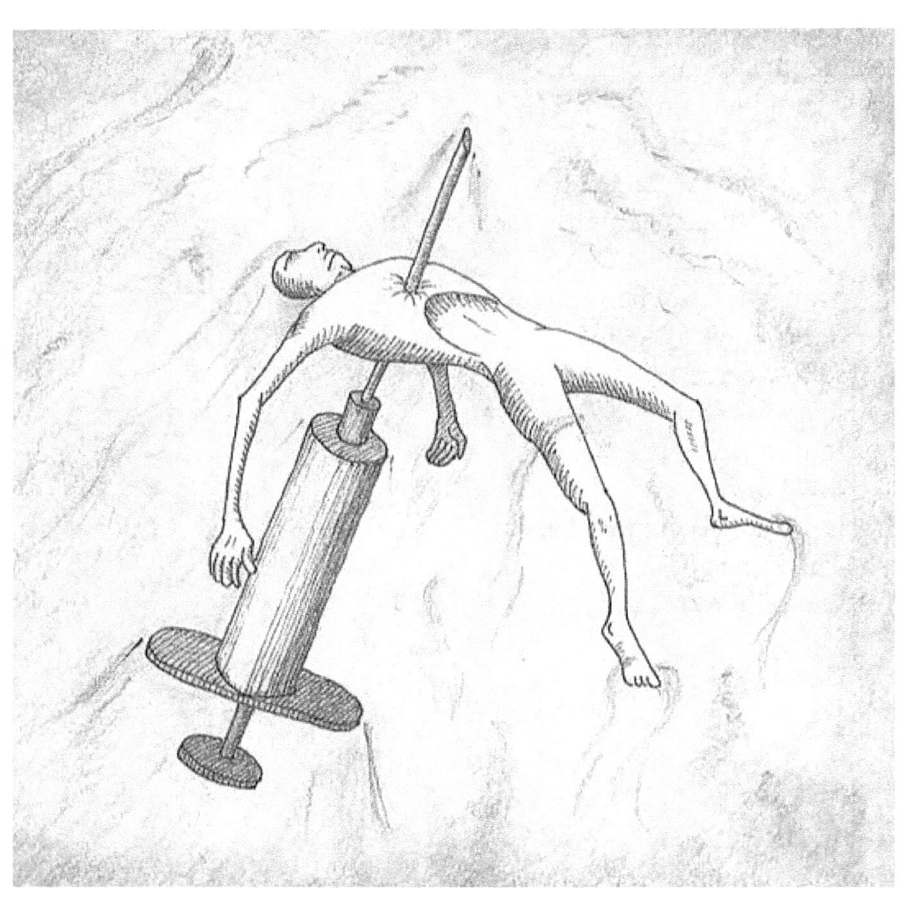

The Cost of Addiction

For many, many years
My heart and soul felt lost
In the hell that I created.
My addiction soon took me into
Despair such as I have never known.
Society would only stare and
Shake their heads in disgust.
My addiction took me
Deeper into total isolation.
I managed to survive
Near death overdoses
And suicide attempts.

I caused my mother many tears
And many fretful nights.
I truly broke her trust
Yet she never did give up.
The drugs now only numb the pain
That never goes away.
As painful as it is to see
Addiction stole my soul and
Sent my life straight
Into the depths of hell.

Greggory Davis

That Gentle Touch

I roamed around in life
Stumbling, failing and losing myself.
A warm gentle touch
Came upon the sweet breeze
From a tender hand
That would always pick mi up.
 My addiction and sin
Took me into the depths of hell.
Isolation and fears in my life
Would let no one enter in.
That warm gentle touch
Coming in upon the breeze, from that tender hand,
Lifted me up once again, from the
Dark and lonely hell that I was living in.
Today I do believe with all my heart
That warm gentle touch
Coming in on the breeze
Is my Lord Jesus Christ
Carrying me through life's craziness
End into eternity.

Greggory Davis

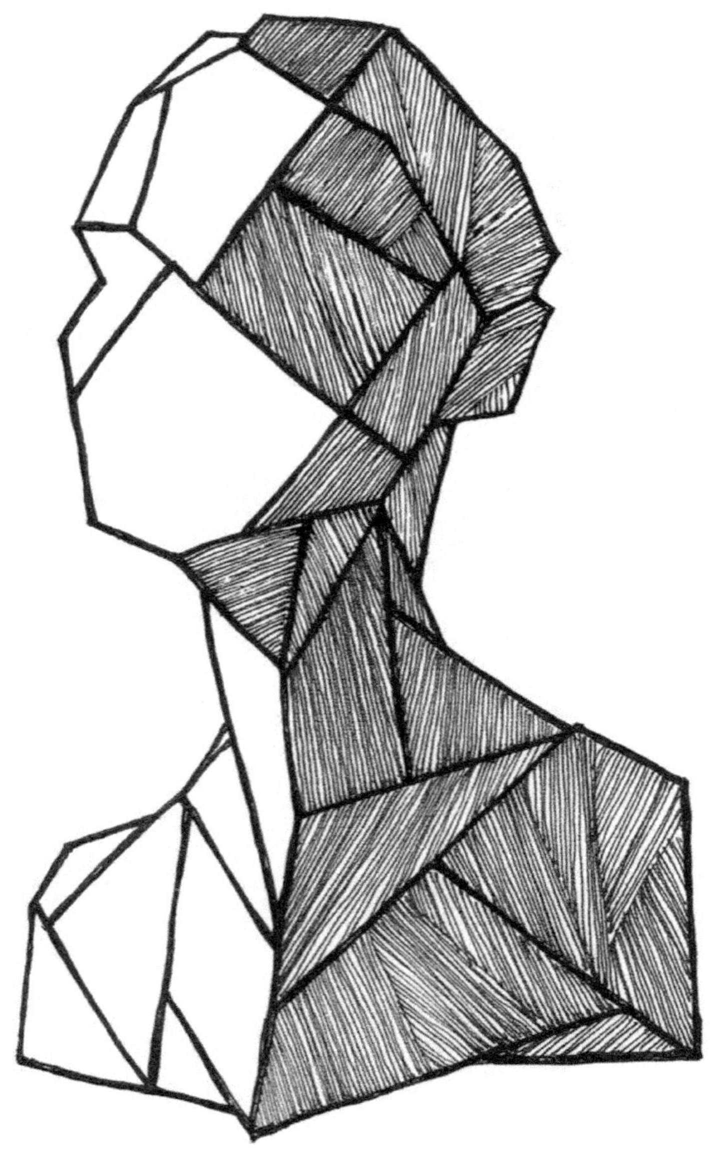

Recovery Bound

Today I sit and ponder
At the way my life has gone.
I've always felt so alone
And kept my feeling deep inside.
When I started getting high
I loved every drug I tried.
I could not face life
The way it was going.
No one was allowed to get close
For I truly feared rejection.
In my quest to be set free
I entered rehab 23
Since the year 1993.
This time it is different,
I'm doing it for me.
I no longer have to beg lie or steal.
Today I can let me feeling show.

I'm no longer just a junkie
Trying only to survive.
Today I am a person with
A voice all of my own.
I choose to live today
"One day at a time'.
I'm finally learning to survive
In recovery from drugs and alcohol.

Greggory Davis

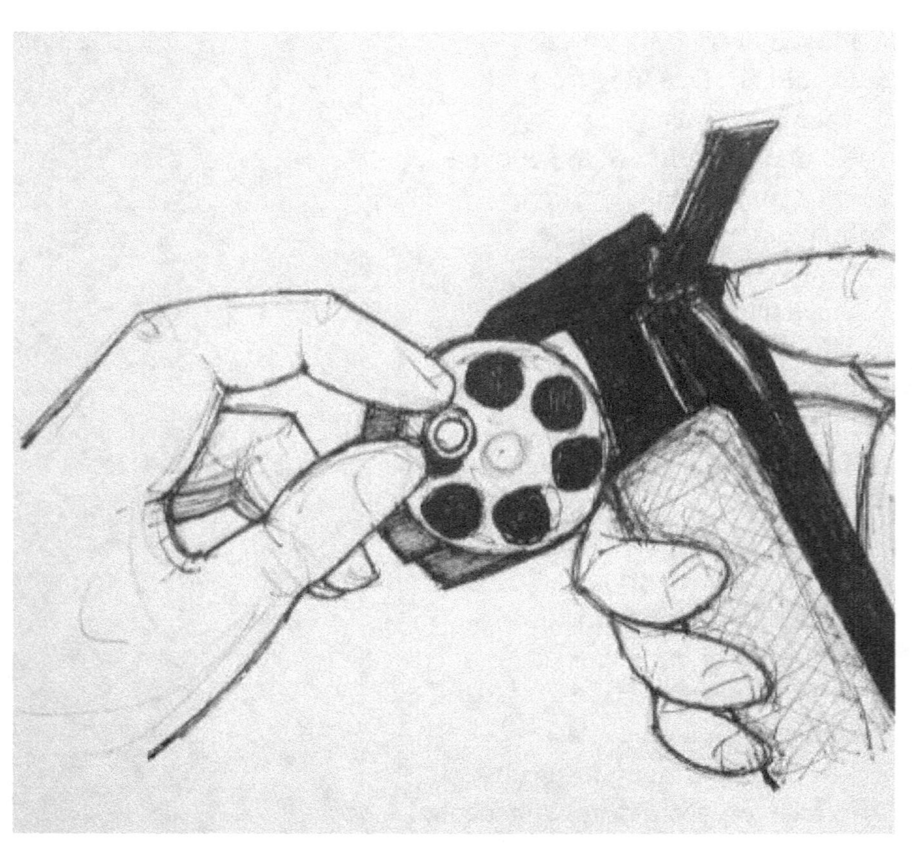

One Bullet in the Gun

We started out as friends
And soon became as one.
Russian Roulette is the game
With one bullet in the gun.

Still you rocked my world
And won my heart and soul.
I shot you into my veins
And took you up my nose.
Russian Roulette is the game
With one bullet in the gun.

What started out as friendship
Soon became romantic.
You calmed my nerves
And confidence you gave.
Russian Roulette is the game
With on bullet in the gun.

With you came overdoses
And once a flat lined heart.
My death I did not fear
I took you back again.
Russian Roulette is the game
With one bullet in the gun.

The time has finally come
For us to part our ways.
My life means more to me
Than that bullet in the gun.
Russian Roulette is the game
That I once played.

Greggory Davis

My Warrior Within

Once tall, brave and proud
My warrior within last the
Fight to my addiction and sin.
Wait, how the hell did they win?

My warrior within is now lost,
Empty, unhappy and so beaten down.
He wound up all alone,
Full of shame, guilt, anger and disgrace.
He turned tricks, and committed crimes
All for his next fix.

Many years later, too tired to fight
My warrior within
Cried out to the Lord.
Pleading for his mercy and grace.
Through his tears, through his fears
My warrior within, finally found hope
Through a drug rehab center
Where people truly cared.

Once again I can stand
Tall, brave and proud
For my warrior within
Is again fighting to win
"One day at a time"
Against my addiction
And sin.

Greggory Davis

My Soul in the Mirror

I stood at the mirror
Trying hard not to stare
At the lost, empty soul
Staring coldly back at me.
Who is that lost, empty soul
With no life left inside?
Dam, it so looks like me,
When did my soul die?

My light had gone out long ago,
My life seemed so dark.
Wait, what's that I see?
It's the light of life
All a glow and so bright.
I've fought long and hard
And the tears I have shed
Brought me back from the dead.

I now stand at the mirror
Staring long, hard and in awe
At a man full of life,
Staring with love
Back at me.

Greggory Davis

My Dark Soul

In my quest to find myself
I found drugs and alcohol.
I fell instantly in love
With how they made me feel.
I no longer had to care
About my values, heart or soul'
For the drugs had me
Totally out of control.
Getting high was I wanted
No matter what it cost.
I'd lie, I'd steal and I'd even
Sell my body and my soul!
Nothing mattered anymore
My body kept craving more.
I kept blaming friends and family
When in all honesty I was to blame.
Now seemed to give a dam
That I felt totally alone.
As long as I stayed high
My shame and anger I could hide.
The gates of hell soon opened wide
With Satan standing just inside
To claim another dark soul
That he had worked so hard to win.

Greggory Davis

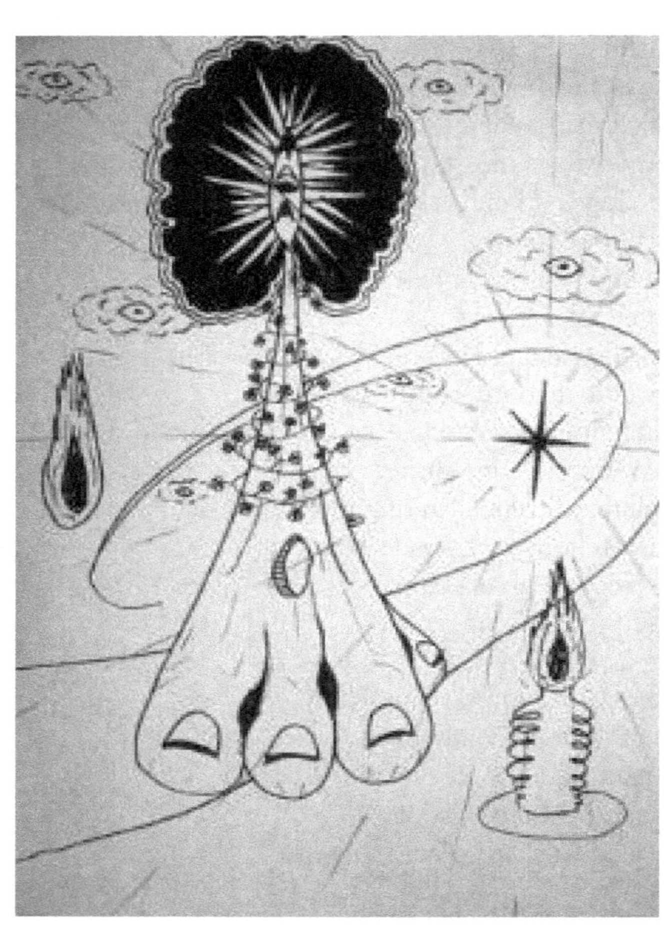

Master Heroin

OH, Master Heroin
My life you have destroyed
And my childhood you stole.
From the moment that we met
You had me all fucked up.

I lied, I cheated, I stole
My body I did sell.
You made me sick as hell
Every day that I'd wake up.
You knew that I would
Soon come running back to you'

You made my friends all I hate me,
My family you chased away.
My soul you came to take.
On the streets you left me
My fate you hoped I'd meet.
Oh my Master Heroin
The time has finally come
For me to take back my life.

And I am going to find out
Just who the hell I am!

Greggory Davis

Just another Cold Day

It was a bitter, cold and windy day
As we stood huddled together
Wrapped in torn and dirty blankets,
Trying to stay warm
In alleys and in doorways.
We passed around a stolen bottle of alcohol
Followed by a joint and cigarette.

As we continued getting high
Our loved ones crossed our minds.
We cheated, stole and sold ourselves
Just to survive on the cold winter streets.
The mission doors are open now.
We follow the line to the door,
Chilled down to the bone,
Praying for a warm meal and bed.
As we approach the door,
We hear them say
"Sorry guys we have no more openings."
As they shut the door they say
"May the Lord keep you warm and safe"

Hopelessly we wander through the streets
Asking God to keep us safe.
We steal another bottle just to make it through
Another lonely day on the
Cold and bitter streets.

Greggory Davis

Jesus Won My Soul

I've walked through life
Facing challenge after challenge,
That always kept me down.
When I would fight to stand back up
I would always see this light
And hear a gentle voice
Calling out my name.

Take my hand, you can trust me,
I've been weighting just for you,
And watching safely over you.
I felt so dam unworthy,
And kept dong life my way.

Finally, I was beaten down,
Addiction had grabbed my soul.
Soon, I reached out
And took that gentle hand.
Satan screamed in pain,
Because Jesus bought my soul
On that horrible beaten cross.

Greggory Davis

Hope without Dope

Once again my life has changed
My head I now hold high.
No longer do I fear my life,
Nor do I walk in shame.

For the 12 Steps of NA
Have saved my ass again.
"One day at a time", I now live.
Today I don't wake up
Needing that morning fix.
No longer do I back out
Nor fear another overdose.
I still have daily struggles
And sometimes feel like giving up.

My daily fight is real
And being clean and sober
Is not an easy road.
But Jesus gives me strength each day
To hold on to one more day of
Hope without dope.

Greggory Davis

Freedom in Christ

I've often wondered why
The Lord would even care
About a lost and evil soul
Such as mine.
I've always walked a thin line
Going between Heaven and Hell.
Satan used my addiction
And all the evil I have done
To win my heart and soul.
I used drugs to forget and to numb the pain
Of life's up's and down's.
My heart was torn between
What is right and what is wrong.
My mind was altered by the drugs
And I doubted that Jesus even cared.
Satan was on his way to
Gaining full control
Of my life, my heart and my soul.
Jesus came and rescued me
When I called upon his name.
His death on the cross and
My choice to follow him,
Has given freedom
To my heart and soul.

Greggory Davis

An Angry Addict

I was angry at the world
Everyone seemed so happy
I had to push them all away.
I could not ever let them know
The horrible pain I felt inside.
My life and soul I handed over
To drugs and alcohol.
My addiction soon took over,
And the anger only grew.
I would rob you and your family,
And con your teens into get high.
I really didn't give a fuck.
I did all kinds of insane shit
Because I needed one more fix.
When my world came crashing down
I truly feared that I would die.
There in the midst of my won hell
I hit my knees in tears
And cried out to the Lord
"How can you love and addict such as I"
If you are really there God
Please I really need you now.
In my heart I heard Jesus say
"my father sent me here
To die upon that cross
To save a soul just like yours."

Greggory Davis

An Addict's Pain

My emotions run wild with
Hate, shame, guilt and anger.
I've tried so hard to let them go
Yet I would hide all of
My tears and my fears.
No one must ever know
Just how much I hated myself.
I always felt lost, empty, lonely and hurt
And I'd blame those who cared
I know deep in my heart
That I am to blame
For my drug use has
Caused all of my pain.
I used them for fun, to forget all my pain,
And to cope with my insane ways.
Now many years later
I'm addict who is fighting
Really hard to put them down
Once and for all.
I had to take a long hard look
At my insane life and
I chose to quit using
As I deserve more in my life
Than the pains of an Addict.

Greggory Davis

A New Life

For many, many years, I wandered aimlessly
Through my life in a daze,
With no idea who I was.
There was no fucking meaning
To life that I was leading.

I use to pray each night
For God to end my life,
I didn't care if I went to heaven or to hell,
I just didn't want live with
All the pain that the drugs and alcohol
Brought into my life each day.

Today, God granted me
A new life in recovery.
I traded in my old life
And walk beside Jesus
For he paid a high price for me.

My tears and fears no longer
Haunt my soul and heart.
Jesus shed his blood on the cross
To give me a new life and
Save my soul from hell.

Greggory Davis

Acceptance

When life seems so confusing
With all the different people we will meet,
While walking down the street.
They may be rich or poor, gay or straight,
Black or white, young or old.
From different cultures we shall come
Searching for a new freedom.
We'll find our lives united
Around the tables of recovery.
We'll try real hard to accept
That we are addicts,
And fix our screwed up lives.
Our prejudices we'll set aside
And accept on another
For who we truly are.
When it is hate we feel
We ask ourselves "Is this fear?"
Please remember this
Acceptance is all it takes
To end this lifelong hate.

Greggory Davis

My Short Autobiography

I grew up in a middleclass family of five. I am the second of three sons born into my parents' life. We lived in Waterford Township, Michigan. My father worked full-time on the midnight shift for General Motors, in Pontiac Michigan. He was also a full-time volunteer firefighter in Waterford. My mother worked as manager in the automotive department for Montgomery Wards. Growing up my parents did everything they could to give us good love filled life. They made sure that we had quality family time, camping out one weekend a month from May through October, we had our family vacations which were usually 2 weeks in November for the deer hunting season. We spent a lot of summer days on the lakes where we learned to swim, water ski, and fish. They supported us in all that we tried to do in life, from school activities, sports and scouts.

While my home life was good, I faced several struggles in life. I sucked at learning, and my school work showed it. I for some reason could not comprehend the lessons and would normally fail most of the tests. No matter how hard I tried, I would just always end up with an average to below average grade. My teachers would tell my parents that I was doing the best I could do in class, and that got me to believe that it didn't matter what I did, I would always just be average so I quit trying so hard and accepted it as it was. I was no good at sports, even though my parents were there supporting my efforts, I gave up trying to go the sports route in life. I don't remember ever having any real close friends growing up. My closest friend was my younger brother. We were always together for the most part.

I was about 12 years old, when I had my first encounter with how evil the world could be. I had been molested by a person that I had trusted and it left me feeling angry, guilty, shameful, and my self-worth suffered also. I never told anyone about it, just tried to avoid that person. I started spending time alone going to the nature center near our house, spending time walking through the woods, kind of trying to figure out who I was now. It was in the woods where I had found sort of a safety area in life that I met several older teens who were shady characters to say the least. But I found that they didn't care what I did, who I was or anything about my past. I was introduced to the world of drugs by this group of so-called friends. My first high was from heroin and weed. I remember it made my feelings numb and I didn't have to feel bad about myself, so I continued to see my new friends and getting high started to become a routine habit. I was somehow able to hide this from my parents for many years.

My second trauma in life happened around the age of 14 or 15. I again faced a sexual assault in life that included being assaulted by the guys I was running around with in the woods. Again, I bottled the feelings, and fears, and never spoke of it to any one for years.

As the years went by, my addiction grew into the one thing that made life crazy for me. I ended up living on the streets of Detroit, where I turned to prostitution, hustling, stealing and doing whatever I had to do in order to survive and stay numb to the reality that my life was going downhill faster than I could deal with. From the age of 12 until the start of my recovery from addiction on October 23, 2022, I lived through a hell that only an addict can understand. During the end of my drug use, I would pray that God would just let me die, not caring if I went to Heaven or Hell. I just didn't want to live anymore. I had my first bad overdose in early 2022, flat lining on the way to the hospital. After several weeks in the hospital, I returned to my addiction. I overdosed a second time and something hit me hard enough to try and find a better way of living. I checked into a drug and alcohol rehab in July of 2022, where I spent 3 months trying to rebuild myself. I faced many demons during the next three months, but must not have faced them enough as I relapsed, overdosed the third time, and returned to rehab on October 23, 2022. I was at this point, beaten down to the point in my life I had to choose to live or die. I spent four months dealing with my past openly and letting my feelings go. I started to truly rebuild myself, and started honestly loving the man I was finding in recovery. Today I no longer hate myself, I can look in the mirror and see the man in the mirror, searching for new hope, for peace and for a better way of life.

Today I embrace my new life without drugs. I am blessed to still have my family (mom, dad and brothers) in my life. My mom is truly special, for she never gave up on me, and she is my solid rock in life today. She is the strongest woman I have ever known. I am also thankful that God never gave up on me, and Jesus Christ holds my life in his hands and as long as I am his lamb, I can do anything without picking up another drug in life. While I can't change my past, and I have no promise of tomorrow, I live for God on day at a time. I hope that my story has helped one person stay clean today. If you are an addict or know and love an addict please know three is hope for recovery. Stay strong and God Bless!